Dear Doft: A Canadian Mennonite farm woman talks to her dead husband

David Waltner-Toews

Published by David Waltner-Toews, 2024.

While every precaution has been taken in the preparation of this book, the publisher assumes no responsibility for errors or omissions, or for damages resulting from the use of the information contained herein.

DEAR DOFT: A CANADIAN MENNONITE FARM WOMAN TALKS TO HER DEAD HUSBAND

First edition. February 22, 2024.

Copyright © 2024 David Waltner-Toews.

ISBN: 979-8224763283

Written by David Waltner-Toews.

Table of Contents

Dear Doft
A Canadian Mennonite farm woman talks to her dead husband

Copyright Page
@ David Waltner-Toews, 2023.
Published by DT Ivanovitch Books, Kitchener, Ontario

Table of Contents

Preface: Who is it that so possesses me?

August 24, 1926, was a beautiful sunny day in the neatly and efficiently planned Mennonite village of Hierschau, Soviet Ukraine. On foot and in horse-drawn wagons, men, women and children came kicking up the dirt and talking down the dusty main street to *Wirtschaft* (farmstead) number 30, the Johann Willms place. Having survived a brutal civil war and famine, they came for bargains, steaming bowls of borscht, and distraction. The Willms kids had already lost two fathers before 1914. Their mother Gertrude, after having hosted the Red Army, the White Army and the Makhnovski anarchists, serving them borscht, bread, and once, cherry dumplings, had died of complications from malnutrition, in 1924. She was 55. Before she died, Gertrude had talked with neighbour Peter Dyck, from number 27 across the way, about emigration to Canada. Now, over the protests of other relatives, the children were carrying on her dream. They could imagine no good future, no interesting story, for themselves in this country. The auction of the Willms and Dyck household goods and farm equipment went well, one beautiful doll even bringing in 18 rubles.

That night, as he found a place to stretch out among the 20 people piled in sleepy heaps around the house, Peter Dyck thanked God for the blessings of the day. God-willing, the eight children of the Willms family (nine including in-law Aaron Wall), along with neighbours Peter and Katharina Dyck and their 10 children, would soon be leaving for Canada. Some of the girls, having returned late from visiting their cousins to say last good-byes, were just falling asleep when Aaron Wall pushed the box with the auction money under their bed.

When the bandits arrived, they surprised the three young men guarding the front door. One was shot, the bullet grazing his scalp, as he ran; the other two tried to claw their way into the house, but the doors were bolted from the inside. The bandits beat them unconscious with their rifle butts. Aaron ran through the house crying "Get the girls up and save your lives! Run for your lives!"

Those who could not hide, fled. Elizabeth Braun (aged 29) took her two younger half-sisters, Aganetha (Nettie, aged 15) and Katharina (aged 17) Willms, by the hand, and led them through a chaotic hell of yells, crashing, and confused people. They ran toward the back of the house, where they heard more shots, and the thump of what sounded like a body falling. They turned back, thinking to hide in the attic, but brother Gerhard (aged 23) barred the way with a shotgun. "If they set the house on fire," he said, "you don't want to be up there. Try the barn." They ran through the passage to the barn, but the bandits were there already, barging into the dark at the far end. The girls slipped in among the horses as the men, coming closer, yelled at them to come out. They made a break for it, crawling under a threshing machine, and then, prying loose a board, squeezed out into the frenzied night, amid the storm of screams and gun explosions, and ran through the garden to the neighbour's house. The girls did not see Elizabeth's little two-year old nephew Jonathan, as he sat, bleeding, calling for help from the hedge where he had crawled to hide after the thieves had beaten him. They did not stop to check the bodies in the yard. They wondered if they were the only ones left alive. When Gerhard fired a shot through the attic window, the bandits panicked and fled.

All except Peter Dyck, who was shot dead, survived, although many were beaten and bloody. Strange for a person to say it so, but even more importantly, the money chest survived (strange, for in some way, by saying so, are we not all reduced to thinking like thieves?). But that money was train tickets, passports, bribes, and a new life. Over the next three days, the kids—including Nettie and Katie's sister Truda, aged

21—scattered to the homes of different relatives. Finally, in secret, older brother Gerhard gathered them into a horse carriage and sped to the train station at Nelgovka.

As agreed, the family gathered in Moscow, from where they took a train to Riga, Latvia. Twenty-three-year-old Gerhard, brother to the three Willms sisters, stayed back, probably because he was deemed of age to serve in the military[1]. The guards at the border took many of their belongings, but they were relieved to be free. From Riga they crossed the North Sea to England, and took a train to Southampton, from where they boarded The Empress of Scotland. In Montreal, Nettie (my mother) said they were "herded into immigration cubicles and sorted out." The kids were sent to Saskatchewan and Alberta, where they worked as farm helpers and house servants.

Unbeknownst to 15-year-old Nettie, her future husband John Toews, my father, was part of that same 1926 migration. He was with his parents and siblings. Later, after her work as a live-in housemaid in Calgary, during the Great Depression, after she gave John one last chance at the railway station: ask or be on your way. Later she worked as a wife, mother, unacknowledged co-writer and editor for her husband, and what was called a help-meet for workers in The Kingdom.

By 1978, at the age of 30, I had never written anything creative with the word Mennonite in it. The past was too much with me. I had left Winnipeg at 19 years of age, vagabonded around the world, wanted to get away from the burden of being a "Russian" Mennonite, all that stuff, to start anew with no baggage. There is always baggage of course, and the heaviest bags are those that are not acknowledged. Your spine begins to warp, trying to bear such a load under your arm, or in an inside pocket, pretending it isn't there. In order to be forgotten, accepted, or even forgiven, something must be remembered. At least once it is acknowledged, a person can figure out how to carry it and still maintain good posture (bend your knees, keep your head up, all that).

When we had our own children, I wanted to pass on stories I'd grown up with, especially the stories told in the home, to private audiences, and not from the pulpits, or in tracts or historical monographs. But, without stirring up all the anger, guilt, angst and cynicism that I associated with some of my upbringing, could I do this? I knew it would need to have food in it, since food was in part what held our culture together. And, since the real history of "Russian" Mennonites[2] was told by women in the kitchen and not the historians in the library, that the voice would need to be female. My formidable aunt Trudawas an obvious choice, along with my own mother and another sister, Katie, all smart women whose dreams were thwarted by patriarchy and global upheavals. But how to give them voice?

In the late twentieth century, the term "performance poetry" was used (some might say co-opted) by certain poets to demonstrate their "originality," this quality being elevated to the realm of the sacred. Performance poetry of course has a long tradition with predates written books, winding its way through oral histories and story-telling of many cultures, from Homer to dub. This sort of poetry has drifted into and out of popularity, and often marginalized from main stream literature into "ethnic" ghettoes as Caribbean dub or American rap. In 2021, performance poetry for the first time jumped into the cultural mainstream with Amanda Gorman's performance of "The Hill We Climb" at the US presidential inauguration. Even then, one could hear critics mutter that this wasn't "real" poetry. Probably the same earnest literary critics who scorned Bob Dylan's 2016 Nobel Prize for Literature.

Until 1969, the year I arrived at Goshen College, a small Mennonite liberal arts college in Indiana, the poems I had written veered wildly between the extremes of sentimental greeting card rhymes, composed for birthdays, funerals, and other similar occasions, and raging, out-of-control laments, which might or might not have been therapeutic. Having been educated in European literature, the poets I longed to emulate included William Blake (for the intense, hallucinatory, iconoclastic, religious content), Dylan Thomas (for the delight in word-plays), and John Donne (for the understated and clever, mix of sex and piety). But where, amid the chaotic upheavals of the late 60s and early 70s, could one find authentic voices for a Mennonite kid from Manitoba, who grew up knowing that music was good, but literature was for "liars and rascals?"

My poetry instructor at Goshen College—the small Mennonite liberal arts college I attended—was Nick Lindsay, son of Vachel Lindsay, the founder of what he called "modern singing poetry" which is one version of performance poetry. Verses are meant to be sung or chanted. Nick, who carried on the tradition of poetry as singing and chanting, was a carpenter from Edisto Island, South Carolina, as well as a poet.[3] I found Lindsay's chanting, hypnotic, incantations puzzling in their points of reference, embarrassing in their raw emotion, and inspiring for their unabashed chutzpah. In some ways, this chanting poetry was perfect for what I wanted: poetry that was directly engaged with what people did every day in their working lives, and which performed better on the stage than on the page. At the same time, I wasn't quite sure how to translate that into something usable in my own writing. I focused, then, on the daily drills Nick required of us, writing in various poetic forms, learning basic techniques, the equivalent of playing scales and Hanon exercises on piano. At the time, with the world around us falling apart, it almost seemed like pointless busyness. It was only after leaving the quarrelsome cosiness of liberal arts academia for a paying job in the dung-and-disease business that I realized how fortunate I had been to have had a carpenter as a poetry teacher.

Although from Lindsay I had learned the craft of building performance poetry, the voice I needed, which certainly wasn't my own, eluded me.

In the end, I was saved by a long poem from Uganda, introduced to me by another Goshen College Professor, Mary Oyer through my wife Kathy, who had taken an African Arts course as a side to her nursing studies. Okot p'Bitek published "The Song of Lawino" in 1966. He wrote in Luo, a decidedly non-mainstream African language, and it was translated, warts and all, directly into English. He called his style "comic singing."

Dancer, drummer, anthropologist, and social critic, he sang recklessly, full of love and therefore without self-censoring his deepest feelings, about the woes of modernization, of men running off to the big city, running after big city women and taking on big city airs, about corruption and infidelity and salvation, a song full of nostalgia, anger, hope, and, what was this—humour? I devoured the book-length tale-telling song at a sitting. That was me. That was my mother. That was, especially, Tante Truda, my mother's sister. That was all of us "Russian" Mennonites. Straight from Luo into English, Mary Oyer meeting Nick Lindsay.

And that, transmogrified, became Tante Tina, straight from Low German, an unwritten language of my parents and ancestors, to English, the language of empire and assimilation. Low German was the "Russian" Mennonite language of the barnyard and kitchen (see postscript "A Note on Language for Dear Doft"). The unwritten mother tongue I had never learned, but whose rhythms and lilts were embodied in my DNA, Low German provided the linguistic structure of the immigrant English I grew up with. And, using this hybrid tongue, Tina became the poetic muse who saved me, who became my poetic voice for a decade, the

1980s, when many men were getting self-censored laryngitis. How could a white middle class male with all the privileges and rights thereto attending have anything important to say at all? How could we get drunk and be miserable and happy without being accused, again, of some form of wrong-thinking or inappropriate feeling?

So I did the only thing I could: I got out of myself, sex change and all. I became an older woman, my mother, my aunts.

The original "Tante Tina's Lament" ended on an upbeat note. So, not only had I managed to write about my Mennonite ancestors, but I had done so with descending into preaching, judgement, recrimination. Tante Tina first made her appearance in a Toronto magazine, "The Canadian Forum" in 1979. I had to laugh at the illustrations added by the magazine editors, which were of Old Order Mennonites in black hats and kerchiefs. My Tina, who came as an orphan refugee to Canada from the Soviet Union in the 1920s, and now lived in Altona, Manitoba, was not such an Old Order or Amish Mennonite. This was another sign, to me, that every label—Mennonite, Christian, socialist, scientist, poet—is both an opportunity and a trap, that every boundary were draw around ourselves is both necessary and is necessarily re-negotiated day by day, fragile, temporary, not to be confused with reality, and often misinterpreted by those around us (especially the non-Mennonites, a.k.a., no matter what their linguistic or culture background as *The Englische*).

In 1986, when I was working in Indonesia, I attended a conference in Singapore of the Commonwealth Languages and Literatures Association titled: "Englishes of the Commonwealth." I performed Tante Tina, and found an immediate sense of camaraderie with the British-Guyanese writer David Dabydeen, who said his own grandmother would tell the same stories, with her own unique brand of English.

In 1993, at the Twentieth Anniversary of the Writers Union of Canada (TWUC), I was asked to read "Tante Tina's Request to put Salman Rushdie on the Missionary Prayer list." Novelist, activist and nature writer Graeme Gibson[4] suggested I do it in costume. At the time, I had never done this. In the service of my art, I went room to room in the dormitory at university where we were meeting, asking if someone had a dress I could borrow. This being a union of writers, already a bit off-kilter just by being scribblers, someone obliged. Then, between the main course and the dessert, I went to the men's bathroom to change, where I was eyed with bemusement by other bladder-emptying men. I was simply introduced as a woman from southern Manitoba. Apart from my moustache, and the sagging breasts made of hand towels, I was told it was very convincing. Well, the light was poor, which helped.

Later, I couldn't recall whose dress I had borrowed, and the next morning I stood up at the AGM and announced that I had a woman's dress from the previous night, but I couldn't remember her name. The response was predictable[5].

After that, to address the confusions in the minds of non-Mennonites as reflected in The Canadian Forum, I (Tina) took to wearing a kerchief and dress, purchased at Value Village in Kitchener. The young woman who sold me the dress didn't bat an eye when I asked her what my dress size might be; just looked me up and down and said, maybe a 14? But some of the customers looked askance when I traipsed out of the closet-sized change room to check myself in the mirror.

Once Tina was out of the closet, she opened a great many conversations, performing on national radio, as well as in churches, bars, synagogues and libraries. She conversed several times with Peter Gzowski, an interviewer with a wide audience on CBC radio. But, more importantly to me, she was able to chatter on in situations that could have just as easily degenerated to slammed doors and shouting matches. She was invited to speak at several conferences of the Mennonite Economic Development Agency, whose members include successful businessmen with whom I have, over the years, had some combative differences of opinion.

In 2008 Tina, in full costume, shared a stage in a barn in Altona, Manitoba (her alleged home town) with a very serious Roland Penner, whose Jewish and Mennonite parents were among the founders of the Communist Part of Canada. I think he was ambivalent about sharing the stage with a Mennonite poet in drag, fearing perhaps that his own story might not be taken with sufficient sobriety of mind. This is a common misconception of course, that serious topics require earnestness.

All my poetry has been written to be performed, which is both freeing, and constraining. It never looks quite as good on the page as it sounds on the stage. Still, like my mother and her sisters, Tante Tina has survived both publication and performance. Along with the poop, disease, and animals of my daily work, and my wife and children (and now grandchildren), Tante Tina grounded me in ways that I had not been before. In giving my mother's generation a voice to speak to the grandchildren, Tante Tina gave me a sense that to honour my father's occupation as a historian, I did not have to study Reformation History. Did I appropriate that voice? More accurately, I would say she appropriated me. I am, after all, the one who puts on the dress and babushka to wag my finger about Trudeau, Salman Rushdie, and the incorrigible stubbornness of men. I am the one who loses my sanity and my rational veterinary and epidemiological poses when she possesses me.

Tina allowed me to accommodate science and story-telling, and helped me regain a voice that was not Tante Tina, but my own, and to find other ways to speak across chasms of culture, belief, science and humanity.

This manuscript represents her last will and testament.

Dear Doft

Sometimes when I am
by the window sitting
and at the crows outside looking,
or looking at nothing, just in my head,
I to myself am talking,
and maybe to Gott
but maybe She only for the worms has ears
and the lilies of the field.
So I am to you this telling
and now you must stay and listen
because you are with the Lord
and you can't your ears be stopping
or me avoiding by to the barn be going.

So was[6], ja? How we old get.

Christmas

Ach, Doft, me it's not
what they want.
It's my stories.
Tell us how it was
they ask me, imagine
Katie and Frieda,
big Haenschen and his Little Haenschen—
ja, that boy has me given a grandson even—
not so long ago just a *Knirps*
but now already with an *Anhaengsel*! These girls
don't like me to say it so,
like they are something hanging on, but with names like
Angela and Mary-Jean, what else can I think?
Such names aren't Mennonite,
like our own Frieda, or Katie, that's sure.
But I love them, ja, they're our Haenschens'.
So is das Leben.
Christmas afternoon the boys still groan
from too much turkey and potatoes,
eat halvah and play *Knipsbrat*
and the kids go out down the riverbank
toboganning, even.
It's the same, like it was.
And before that, even,
Weinachtsabend, after the children's program
at church—you know Little Haenschen
even with his hair so long
they let him read a scripture? praise God—even then,
before the plates for each child
under the tree go, we all sing,

"*Welchen Jubel, Welche Freude*"
so nothing much new under the sun comes.
Maybe my wrinkles only are new.
Now they want stories,
how I walked to school in snow,
they want *Russlaenda* stories
from their Oma.
Once, I tell them, we didn't all think
we could save the world.
That the Lord's work was.
Now even the girls go to college,
and what is coming of that?
A world without borscht and *Rollkuchen*
is not worth saving,
but what do they know of that?
Then I tell them about how one time
the Makhnovists, the bandits,
they came to our house in the Molotschna.
Everyone they would kill, they said, but Mutti
had borscht in a big *Topf* steaming,
and the men when they must choose
between their guns and a spoon for soup,
every time the spoon wins.

The soldiers ate themselves *sat*[7]
and went away, so you see? The Lord provides.
Our boys like that story,
but the *Anhaengsels* are not so sure.
Then I tell them,
Well that was my *Weinachtswuensch*,
where is yours? Well our girls can sing
a duet—in English—what can you do?
"The Holy City,"

so I have to take out my handkerchief.
And even Big Haenschen, you know,
living in that new house with an *Englische Frau*
he can still say:
Da war einmal ein Mann
Er hatte eine Pfann
Die Pfann war ihm zu heiss
So ging er auf das Eis
so I am happy.
And little Haenschen the grandboy with the hair
he can sing with the guitar:
Haenschen klein ging allein
in die weite Welt hinein...
So there we sit in the *Grautestov*,
Big Haenschen in his fancy shoes
and his boy Little Haenschen in bluejeans
and the *Anhaengsels* with *Englische* names even.
Who would say we *mennonitisch* are?
How we think, even,
is all *aufgemixed*.
Big Haenschen has his head all full of Conservative,
and Little Haenschen preaches the gospel socialists
but you can still see it,
it's the same, how they walk,
the real Mennonite way,
like bringing in the cows...
except maybe too much sometimes
what was once on the boots clinging
now from the tongue falls, ja?

Tent Pegs

After the *Weinachtswuenschen*
the children are outside going
in the snow, but once the stories in my head
are starting, how can I stop them?
They are like a train
and then I am down sitting
in the green chair and my eyes close
and I am remembering the gate in Latvia
how on the train the soldiers came.
At each seat they are stopping.
Papers, they are papers wanting.
And things. Where is that samovar from?
Did you steal it?
And then they are taking it.
Or they are saying, these papers are not right.
And then Fred Peters from the train must go
and Mrs Peters and the girls are weeping,
please, please.
When they are by me standing
where I am with my brother Nick,
a squeal there is, in my heart, like a piglet
through the mud schlepping,
everywhere splattering.
So, running away from home?
one of them is saying
No mummy and daddy?
Why not here be staying?
We can take care of you.
One of them is my cheek touching and laughing
but the other one, he is asking,

What are you reading?
I read the Bible. It is all
I am needing.
Ah so many good books
you are not reading. They laugh.
One is me on the breasts touching.
So many good stories you are missing.
I am about the story of Jael thinking
in the Old Testament,
how she her body used,
to bring the enemy into her tent, even,
and how she a tent peg used
his brains out to be poking,
how many stories
these soldiers are not knowing.
And then we through the gate are.
Look, look, said Nick, we are free.
And I am about the border-guard thinking.
In Canada, I have heard, the Indians are tents having.
So, I am thinking, they must tent pegs have.
And I was wishing I already could be there
in Canada, a safe country,
with tent pegs.

On the Ocean to Canada

When I am from my *Mittagschlaf* upgewaking
I first am not remembering
where I am, but the children are more stories wanting.
Some things, dear Doft,
I cannot tell them.
Tell us about the whale, they are saying,
and the bear. Those I can be telling.
Doft, you are already that story hearing from me, ja?
Many times. And now you are with the Lord
so you are all the stories knowing
if they true are even, or if I am just
making up my remembering.
From Southampton, we on a ship were,
so big I from one end
to the other could run
from skinny Fred Penner
until he like a sad tree
bent over was, finally,
all *ausgepoosted.*
At night, in my dreams,
Mutti was with me,
not dead yet, and we still
in Russia were.
She is in the kitchen
by a steaming *Topf.*
and my body for *Kertofel* borscht
is aching.
When I am awake,
up and down we are on the grey water heaving.
I have the story of Jonah read.

Whose fault is this is, they are asking,
the people on the boat.
The whales to me are calling.
I am my dinner over the railing upthrowing.
They are wanting more, those whales.
My heart have I already to Jesus given,
so I can't give it to the fish.
More pieces of food from my mouth are flying,
like swallows to the barn, swoop and down.
It is not enough for the whales.
The Lord is my body wanting, like Jonah.
Over the edge the waves are up-reaching.
Their white fingers catch me and take me.
In his cold salty bosom
the Lord holds me,
so quiet so cold and then so warm,
so still.
And then, from the middle of the green light
God, like a great black bear,
a big furry bear, is coming.
Then I am again on the ship,
under a prickly warm blanket
with cream and red and green and black and yellow stripes,
and my brother Nick
is into my mouth potato soup spooning.
And beside me is standing
a shaggy black dog
from the New Found Land.

The Bear in Alberta

I was alone, once, at the farm
in Namaka, after we are from Montreal
on the train coming, ja, before, long before
we to Altona moved yet,
before even we were married
Nick and me have
for room and board at Peter Warkentin's farm
been working. Everyone but me was to young people's
at church gone. I was sick,
my body hot all over, so hot
like when the flies in the summer kitchen
sit on the cutting board, wheezing,
and with their little black hands
are rubbing spit on their faces, so hot.
But outside it was spring,
Alberta spring, with snow ja?
And downstairs snuffling and grunting I could hear,
banging and crashing in the kitchen,
and glass breaking,
and I am thinking the cream is spilling,
and the honey pail over-falling.
I am wondering,
has God come again?
To the back door
like the black dog, like on the sea,
when I saved was?
I am here! I am wanting to say.
I am here up the stairs, the second bedroom!
But my voice is scratchy
and God is not me hearing.

Later such shouts and yammering,
when everyone from Young Peoples
is coming back. The honey!
The whole pail of hard white honey
from Grande Prairie!
And the fish Nick has
in the irrigation ditch *ge-caught*!
All gone!
And then fat Mrs. Warkentin
like pillows full of prickly wet feathers
in her stiff Sunday dress
is hugging me,
Oh you are safe,
lieber Gott, you are safe.
But God is not back-coming.
And Nick has me getold
that there was a hungry black bear
and everyone is happy
I am not dead
even if the fish and the honey
are all gone.

How we are Meeting

Ach, and now the children
are wanting to know
how we are meeting, Doft.
What can I be saying?
Some stories I can only
you be telling.
They are not for children's ears.
You a *Schlingel* were,
since long already
before we married,
but this you later forgot, I think.
Should I be telling them?
This I am not sure.
I have been telling them
that we have ourselves found
in Bible School and have been married
when the dust storms were thick in the air
and the wind like a choir of chicken manure
from the coulee was singing.
My white dress and your navy suit and our faces
all were grey, so in the pictures
we already old looked yet.
And then I am remembering
how our family came once over to dinner
at your house at the Namaka farm
all *aufgedressed* from church,
do you remember?
close around the table,
the steak in sauce so good
from in the oven all through church baking

you could eat it with a spoon,
and potatoes mashed with a *Loch*
in the middle for gravy.
We were all smelling so much
we could hardly hold ourselves for eating,
and your Papa asks you to pray
with your brother Pete.
I am thinking you will say
Segne Vater diese Speise
Uns zur Kraft and Dir zum Preise Amen
but together you sing
"Eetle ottle black bottle
Eetle ottle out Amen"
and then burst out laughing like horses
blowing through the nose.
I am not even knowing
what that rhyme is meaning.
Your Papa so angry was
he said nothing
but dragged you boys by the neck
out to the barn
so we the cries couldn't hear.
And even after your Mutti prayed,
Elsie and I were still ashamed
for being girls and thinking you boys
did it for us, to show off, ja,
so we into our plates looked
and haven't much eaten.
And there was the time an *Englische* preacher
from the city came and spoke
about tithes and offerings
for the *Konferenz*, and you have your tie

into the collection plate put.
They are *tithes* saying, not ties,
but this you knew already, ja.
And once when you already in Bible School were
Bob Friesen from Winnipeg came to visit
to the farm and you let him ride
the one horse who loved the barn
more than anything,
so when they went out it was slow
like going to the front to get saved,
but coming back
it was fast like a pig running
and when they through the door of the barn
came back-galloping,
the Friesen boy his pants filled,
and you were in the straw laughing.
But this story I have not shared.
What good can come from that?

The First Move

I have been telling the children
how, after we have married,
we were to Manitoba from Alberta moving.
My brother Nick has a farm in Coaldale *gebought*
with our money, a nice farm with sugar beets and
Indians to dig them up, ja.
We will be milk cows in Manitoba having,
you said, Doft. Just like before, in Russia.
We are by that old Ford going, the truck
you remember ja? All our things we have
geschlepped over the prairies,
and all around, flat, flat just like in Russia,
and the sky so big,
and the sun pouring down
like hot butter sticking on everything
until we have to our piece of land been coming.
There were trees, so many stones and trees.
It was the only land we could afford
because we our money used up to help Nick,
but this his wife later forgot, ja?
So hard we worked! my brother's wife is saying,
so the Lord is us blessing.
Ha, ja with our money she is *geblessed.*
And she so stingy is, like a wooden clothes-pin,
I think she must be conservative voting.
So was, ja? we have dug and chopped to make a place
for the garden, and for the cows and the horses,
and for the house and for the barn.
At night Doft's back has so much been aching
from all the trees down hacking, and his arms

were from the black flies and the mosquitoes bloody.
The horses have their feet up-lifted
one by one, up, and then put them down,
like they are feeling if they are still are there,
after the roots up-pulling,
the roots with all their might
at the stones grabbing,
and at last into the dirt falling,
like old white hands with artheritis.
In the Fall when we the fields over-looked,
our hearts almost breaking were,
like ice, it was so hard. In October already
the snow came shrieking with the wind,
into our home, through the cracks
by the door, by the window,
little white foxes of snow in-creeping,
on the quilt sleeping, wet spots making,
little white feathers under the blanket
into our stiff bones poosting.
And then I tell the children, now I am tired
from story-telling
and need to be resting.
But I am lying then in bed,
and the thinking will not stop,
how the more hard we worked,
the more the Lord blessed,
the more pious you were,
until how many were the cows,
and how big was the tractor,
and the word of the Lord,
all were the same.
The two girls Frieda and Katie came

and could *zucker Platz* make
but you had no *Platz* except for Haenschen
who came after,
and then only in the barn.
At Christmas,
we still were singing
"*Nun ist sie erschienen, die himmlische Sonne,*"
and in the black stove
we have from the Eaton's store in Winnipeg *gebought*,
the chopped trees have been *ge-crackling*.

Our Boy Haenschen

But after, ach Doft, what has happened?
That last time our boy Haenschen from the barn called,
Come quick to see, so you through the door went
and down the milk pail on your head
is spilling—after the wide pants and the dancing
that was the last thing.
You so hard hit him with the stick
until the blood came,
and after Haenschen for sure
nothing of the farm wanted,
and in his fancy *Hosen* to the city went
and from church *ist abgefallen*.
And you were sitting on the milk stool
and nothing saying.
Was war zu sagen?
Haenschen was a fool,
that's sure, but just like you,
this I can say, ja, now
when you are with the Lord
and he is not home.
Haenschen in the city
would go strutting, like a chicken
in his pink shirt
and plaid, big-bottomed hosen.
When he was little,
his bottom was like a zwieback.
His little buns I spanked
and how he crowed!
But then his tongue he wagged at me
and said I was ignorant.

He said farmers have no brains,
they should all be businessmen.
He said farm girls don't know how to walk
and I a steak don't know how to barbecue.
Oh his heart was full of cold borscht,
and his words were like sour cream.
Don't called me Haenschen, he said.
My name is John.
Do I not know my son's name?
Did we not for six nights
about that name argue already yet?
You are Abe wanting, I think.
On Wednesday night
the young people went to church
even Katie and Frieda.
They were *Platz* eating and testimonies giving.
The girls had long golden hair.
Their cheeks were rosy from harvest
and dresses covered their knees.
When the young people together were singing
it was heaven above and earth below
with sopranos and basses.
But he to the city dancing went.
His girl friend has red grease *gesmeared*
on her lips. Her hair cut and curled was,
and her knees were bare
like a young calf.
When they were dancing
sometimes, even upstairs
in the bedroom I could hear,
their legs were noodles
and the music was a tractor.

The girl friend said it was not a shame
a woman her hair to be cutting.
She was saying Mennonites are like Hutterites
and had never heard of *Rollkuchen*.
Haenschen said she was a modern girl.
He said we must speak *Englisch* to her
because she to the United Church was going.
He was saying Low German is a pile of manure.
Ach Doft, no wonder
you in the barn stayed.
Haenschen did not listen.
We are poor, he said.
We do not know how people are money making.
He wanted to be rich, like the *Englische*,
and from *Mannagruetze* to save us all.
In the barn, the cats were mice eating,
and for milking time were waiting.
When you were coming in
I was dinner serving on a china plate.
But Haenschen always angry was.
You know this. Just like you, ja?
On New Year's Eve
we were going to church at night,
and on Easter
when the sun was rising
we were singing "Up from the Grave."
Haenschen came late to church on Easter,
after sunrise service,
and was at the back sitting.
On New Year's Eve
he was gone dancing.
He did not even come the children to hear

on Christmas Eve.
I remember when he was still a little *Bengel*
he was a wise man in the play.
My heart so heavy was,
all those years,
thick as *Glums*.
I told him, "If you come home
my heart will rise, light and sweet.
I will make you *Porzeltche* for breakfast
and every morning the New Year
we will celebrate."

Ich weiss einen Strom

But he was by then gone.
Katie and Frieda
they gave me some comfort.
But for you there came only work,
and no blessing.
Only once I remember were you hitting me
when I something said
but after you just stayed
from the house.
And then came the stroke.
We had to take you to the bathroom
and from the bed uplifting
and every day the Bible reading.
Always you to the wall looked only.
You had no tongue. But what was
in your head, I do not know.
Once Haenschen came back
and by the bed stood
but you two *Schlingels*
were not talking,
like two old *Pfeffernüsse*
to crack your teeth on,
sitting after Christmas alone
on a kitchen plate.
It is past the time for eating
and they sit there only
remembering for you
that here the family once was.
At the funeral around the open box
we have stood for the picture,

Haenschen and me and Frieda and Katie.
I am thinking,
so bad it wasn't,
I wouldn't it again do.
I am remembering
that sometimes, you still had room for me, ja.
One time, after we
already children had, you are wanting
from your bed to mine to be coming.
But before, you were wanting me all naked
to see, even. Why, I was wondering,
so you are knowing where the old milk bags
are hanging? So you don't miss them
when your hands come to squeeze?
And you were saying: Just to see,
like God is us making,
Then you your pyjamas
are down pulling, and my white woollen nightie
with the pink flowers on the collar is
in a soft puddle falling by my feet.
We are looking each other up and down.
Our bodies wrinkled maps were,
all the places we have been, with rivers
and coulees and bits of bush and that floppy thing
by the cliffs hanging, with the Crimea and Altona
after the sunflowers are picked already,
and the old Namaka farm in 1931
before Altona,
the horses with their saddle backs
and hat rack hips,
and frayed grey blankets
hung over them to dry.

And then I was saying,
Well that is enough of that already yet.
So we have our night clothes been
putting on again and you have your rubber thing
put on and into me slipped, so slippery
I am surprised, like the clay road
to the post box
when the snow melts.
In the morning I was seeing
you have your rubber envelope washed,
and on the line by the tub
to dry have hung. So,
you were thinking maybe you will
again down the old road be coming.
And me, when I the onions was chopping,
thought, ja, maybe, maybe,
another trip to the post box
But dear God,
I am for no more letters hoping.

The Kommunists

After Christmas Little Haenschen and his *Anhaengsel*
are visiting and wanting to know more
about our days in Russia.
Ja, I tell them, our days were like grass,
and the wind passed over
and all our great works were gone.
This we should remember.
But we, we forgot.
Even in Prussia, before Russia,
when they have us *upgerooted*
and we to Russia were trekking,
we were thinking
how those Ost Prussians were missing us!
Who would feed them now?
Who would boats make for them?
And Catherine the Great she was
us welcoming with arms
as big and full of milk as Abe Friesen's cow.
And when the Kommunists have come
and have us away *gesent* for being good farmers.
And German speaking, Little Haenschen says,
Ja, I say like Goethe and Schiller, or Bach,
or even Friedrich Engels,
German-speaking.
So we to Canada are coming.
Little Haenschen has me *getold*
that the government
the Indians has sent away
so we the land can have, like the Cossacks
who Catherine has taken away in Russia

to make for us room.
This I was not knowing.
But what was there to do, then,
when I was just a girl, and no mother and father
and no country where I can speak
or understand,
and all was so strange.
But after they have us sent away,
I think the Kommunists are missing us too,
even if we were German speaking,
because they have dirt now
and no farmers,
like gums with no teeth.
And here in Canada
after all the stumps were *out-ge-pulled*,
like rotten teeth, brown and twisted, the roots
have there been lying,
the furrows like torn gums.
And only after many years,
cows, but bony as Leviticus,
and sunflowers.

What I am Not Remembering

In the evening after the story-telling,
I have been TV watching on the green sofa
with Little Haenschen
and his *Anhaengsel* Angela
in her blue jeans, and her flannel shirt
with some buttons open.
Then he has me been telling how one time,
when he was still just a little *Knirps*
we were together TV watching,
when his mother Mary-Jean and Big Haenschen out were,
I think Mr. Diefenbaker to hear.
On the TV we have the old Doukhobour women seen
up to the front of the political *Konference*
walking, like Mennonites, one foot in front of
the other, like they think they are somewhere going,
maybe to get saved,
and then they are their dresses for Mr. Diefenbaker
off-taking. Oh *so was*! From the back
they are like big lumps
of *Zwieback* dough, ja?
Such commotion!
So I am to Little Haenschen saying,
I would never such a thing do.
No, Oma? No. Never.
Those women their dresses off to be taking
like that, in front of the politicians,
it is like pearls before swine throwing.
But this I am not remembering,
that I would such a thing say to Little Haenschen.
And then I have to the kitchen for tea gone

my memories up to waken.

Rudy Wiebe and the Kommunists

So when I am back from the kitchen coming
I am wanting the subject to change,
so I am down-sitting
with the TV off and am saying,
Let me tell you now how once
Rudy Wiebe has the Kommunists been saving.
This many people do not know.
One time in the Molotschna when
the Revolution was—
this picture, see? My mother is there,
but she already dead was in this picture.
There were Red soldiers and White soldiers
and the Makhnovists who were a black flag waving
and the Mennonites in the *Selbstschutz*,
who just hello waved with Wilma Thiessen's laundry.
They not fighting were,
only self defending by shooting and
very fast running and then being shot.
Always Mutti has soup *gemade*
for everyone, no matter what colour,
red or white.
Rudy Wiebe was one time the kitchen rug out-shaking
for my mother. He visiting was
and something for his soup he needed to do.
Mutti wasn't borscht for nothing giving.
But the Reds they are seeing him waving and thinking
he is with the *Selbstchutz*, so Tolstoy
himself is coming and after Rudy running.
No, you are right, maybe.
Was it Trotsky?

The Kommunist, ja? that one, through the barn
and over the river chasing. He is wanting
Rudy Kommunist to be making or to shoot.
But it is April and the ice on the river has a hole cracked
in it like the old toilet seat behind the house,
slippery and cold just like that,
so Trotsky is through falling.
Plumps, just like that. Nick has once almost been
in-slipping like that even.
Not in the river. In the outhouse.
Then Rudy the cries hears:
Help! Help me comrade!
and is turning and him helping
from the hole. Just like in the Martyr's Mirror,
the story about Felix Manz.
We have soup from Felix the cat made
after the Revolution. But that is a different story.
And after they are to Mutti's house
for soup coming.
Then Trotsky is to Mexico
going, because there are so many Mennonites
and he is the soup so much liking and at home
to be feeling. He has there I think a Petkau girl *gemarried*.
Or that was maybe Tolstoy.
Sometimes I am too old
and I mis-remember.
That is how history is made,
from all our mis-rememberings.
My mother is in the evening lying down,
and in the morning she is not up-getting.
My Uncle Fritz is looking.
The Lord has come for Mutti, he is saying

but I have already
for the picture-taker paid. This he has done
because Nick and I will be to Canada going,
and everyone else is behind staying,
so we a picture are needing. But Mutti with the Lord is.
Was ist zu tun?
We are the navy dress on her pulling
and the Sunday hat with the flowers
on her planting,
and Nick and me are her upholding.
So now we the picture have,
all my life to remember.
Ja, my mother is dead in this picture.
A good picture, Ja?
She doesn't even look dead.
So ist das Leben.
I am wondering now
what has to Rudy Wiebe happened?
And Angela is saying he is books writing
about Mennonites and Indians.
And when I am again to the kitchen
going to bring some fresh buns
and they are thinking I don't hear,
Angela is whispering,
Oh let me your buns be squeezing,
and you can inside my shirt slip
down the smooth shell-belly
to the soft-bearded oyster,
and then your liquid pearls are outcoming, ja?
I think she is mocking, ja?
But then the next Christmas
they have been *ge-married.*

So was, how the Lord works.

Some Mennonites Are Not Smart

Let me tell you, Doft,
not all the Mennonites are like us smart.
Do you remember my cousin Jake Peters?
After twenty years in the mission field in India
he is home-coming to Coaldale in Alberta,
and is to the CBC Check-up program calling,
and for everyone to hear is saying,
he a solution is having
for all this political problems yet.
It is too many immigrants, he is saying.
Ja, he says, I think we should all the *Englische* people
be sending home who are speaking funny
so we can't understand.
Then we can the country be starting over.
The Chinese first, they are from Hong Kong coming
thinking they can anything buy here,
my Truda tells me from Vancouver.
Even the government they are thinking they can buy.
Well maybe it's so, ja?
And Mr. Mulroney, he Irish was
and they are fighting always and drinking
so they for sure should be home going
with their music fiddling on the TV also.
The Indians, too, the ones from India.
Jake Peters is saying, they are here coming
and so hard working they can buy the Thiessen's
farm in Coaldale, ja, George Thiessen whose father
was killed by the Bolsheviks,
how can that right be?
And the other Indians,

who are sugar beets picking
and beer drinking
they can be back going to the bush.
And the Ukrainians they are having their own place now
with the Kommunists gone
where they can go. It is not necessary for them
here to be complaining.
Even from Quebec the French-speaking *Englische*
Jake Peters wants to send home, because he can't *versteh*
them at Thiessen's Supermarket in LaSalle.
They are building monuments, he says, and stadiums
that are down falling, like Stalin's even!
They are Kommunists and drug smokers,
not like Dueck's Construction in Plum Coulee.
So he thinks they should be home going also,
to France. We don't need such monuments here.
And the British, they are speaking funny
like the queen, and they are having their noses in the air,
like they have been behind the barn walking.
Ja, my cousin Jake is saying,
they should all go home, all the *Englische*,
or maybe we can them in those jails be putting
that Mr. Toews from the MB church is wanting to build.
Mr. Toews, Jake is saying, yes I am for him voting
because he is this understanding.
But no, not the Mennonites, Jake has said,
we should not them away be sending
except maybe the *abgefallener* ones
who are not believing.
They can again to Russia go,
to be with the unbelievers,
but me, Jake is saying, after doing the Lord's work

with the heathen so many years
and all the churchly Mennonites,
we should here be staying.
This is our promised land!
Where else is there to be going?
All these things Jake is speaking, I have heard him
on the radio, the CBC even.
Such a cousin!
Jake is even once me telling he thinks
Saddam Hussein the antichrist is,
and I am answering that I think he is *aufgemixed*.
George Bush the antichrist is, or that preacher Robertson,
because he pretends to be good
and then makes evil. I am thinking Jake
his Bible is not knowing very well.
And when I am saying this to him,
Jake has the phone *upgehanged*, already yet!

Phone in to the Radio Talk Show

So then I have also to call to the CBC
to the Check-up Show
so *Englische* people should not be so *aufgemixed*
about Mennonites.
Hello? I am calling. Is this the radio?
The talk-in show?
Ja, it's me, Tina again.
Like a pig this thing squeals.
Turn my radio down? Ja. Just a minute. O.K.
Ja, now I think the Russian
invasion of Grenada—pardon?
ja, I mean the American invasion
in Afghanistan—no, ja,
so much invasions I am now confused
but you know what I mean,
like the British when they came to Manitoba
when Louis Riel was here.
That's when the Harry Dick family
from our village in Russia came
but then they went to Mexico,
because here it was all so *Englisch*, you know?
But now his children
are coming back. Better *Knacksaut* here
I say, ha ha. Ja. Altona is the sunflower
capital of Canada. Harry Dick,
he was my mother's uncle.
Tante Kate, she stayed here.
Twelve children, she told Uncle Fritz,
I'm not dragging them to Fernheim
just so we can our tongues in *Plautdietsch* be wagging.

But some, like the Peter Dicks,
they went too and liked it.
No, I don't think they went to Grenada.
But Harry Peters, when he left Russia,
he came through Afghanistan,
and his children are now missionaries in India.
Ja, what I am saying,
we are more tongues needing in this place,
not fewer. And even French sometimes
like Mr. Trudeau.
Ach, Doft, you have told me once
I am Mr. Trudeau loving too much and
he thinks I would like to kiss him,
or to run away with him even.
Well, maybe it's true
and I am sad,
because there are no more politicians
I am feeling like kissing.
He the last one was, ja?
When we first came to this country
the Liberals were letting us in.
And when I am old,
Mr. Trudeau has me a check given
for old age pension. No one has such a thing
heard before in Coaldale or Altona.
Now all the lazy people want only
to speak in one tongue
like before Babel, but the Lord knows
this is only for money-making good.
For the borscht, the more things go in
the better the eating.
Ach, ja, what do I know,

but when the Holy Spirit came
and everyone was in tongues speaking
they did not all babble the same.
They only understood each other.
Already each tongue
their own country wants,
but those people they have
visions only like a rooster.
But no one listens to an old lady
anymore, ja? So when we each
are sitting alone, speaking to ourselves
in our own tongue, like Mr. Janzen
who lives in the Old Folks home
and who always into his soup mumbles,
maybe they will remember me,
and Mr. Trudeau even,
and they will see, even if a man sometimes
wrong is, it is good to have someone
around to be giving a kiss, ja?
Pardon? Ja, O.K., I'll be short.
I have been forgetting that I still
on the radio am.
What my idea is,
I think they should all come back
to Manitoba—pardon?
Ja, I don't care, the Russians, the Americans, the Harry Dicks,
whoever. My Tante Frieda, she's still in Russia,
at Alma Ata, and Lydia Franz's boy Fred,
he lives in America, in Fresno.
So you see?

Just One More Thing

Okay, I am on the radio still, ja?
Just one more thing, very short,
are you still listening?
I have for you another request
someone on the missionary prayer list
to be putting.
The last time it Salman Rushdie was
who the Lord we asked to be saving
because He through Mister Rushdie like a leaky pail
into the world was coming.
I was thinking then about how John Friesen
has once a letter in Russia written,
during the time of Stalin,
and after, how they took him away
just as he the Bible was reading
at the supper table,
and his wife Elsie and the five children
have him never seen again.
Elsie has told me that John the parable
of Jesus was reading about the vineyard
rented to the workers who all the servants
of the owner killed, even the very son,
and then John told how we are the earth are renting
from God, and when He comes to ask,
well, How goes it?
what can we say, ja?
And then the Kommunists have come
and John has been taken away
and then they have prayed,
and then they have *Schnetki ge-eaten.*

They were *fleisch Piroshki* wanting
but after Stalin's famine
no one had meat.
And I have told Elsie
that God is in that story,
and how much Jesus is stories loving.
Ja, the truth comes to us that way
and we can eat *Schnetki* and life is going on
even then, ja? That is why Stalin and the Ayatollah
and even some Christians
do not like stories so much,
because they think maybe God
is in the story hiding,
like meat in a *fleisch Piroshki*,
and when we the buns are opening,
God is on us checking to ask,
how are we caring for the beautiful vineyard?
This they do not like,
that maybe God is looking,
and that is why I was the church asking
Mr. Rushdie on the missionary prayer list
to be putting.
And the Lord has answered as He promised
even where two or three are gathered
with some fresh borscht and *Zwieback*,
and Mr. Rushdie was then saved even if his stories
not always so good are,
and then we have eaten...
Hello? Hello?
Ach, Doft, they are saying
they want to hear from the listeners
but when I am calling

they have on me *upgehanged* already.
All day I talk to the radio
and even they do not listen.
And now I have forgotten who we
should be praying for. So many ja?
So many are needing it.

Bone-in Bean Soup

Na, ja, on Saturday
Little Haenschen is calling.
He is wanting to learn how
Bohnensuppe to be making.
This is not from a book coming
I am saying.
You come to my place
and I will be showing you.
It is better also for me
to be company having.
I am making him the onions chop
and he is watching how I the ham-
bone in the four-quart *Topf* am cooking—
two or three pounds of *gesmoketeh* ham
in water with two onions.
The onions are making me cry! he says.
I am saying, every day something is making me cry,
even with no onions. Who is for poor people crying?
And for those who no ham-bones
are having? So then we three cups
of fresh green beans are cutting
and potatoes into little cubes chopping
and carrots shredding and into the soup they go.
Then Little Haenschen
has a joke me been telling
about *Bohnensuppe.*
I think maybe it is not so funny
a joke to be explaining to Oma
auf Englisch, slowly, but the boy is good
and says that beans are *auf Deutsch Bohnen,*

which I am knowing
and he is saying the bean soup is having
the ham with the bone in
and we are saying it like bone-in soup,
and then he is about those *Schlingels*
in Ottawa and Washington saying
how they are bones in the head having,
and all the *Dummheiten* they are doing
and saying this from the Bible comes.
They are saying we should more jails be making
for the poor people, ja?
If we are not jails making,
and people in them putting,
then who can we be visiting and comforting
like in the Gospel of Matthew
to show how good we are?
And if we are not someone bombing,
then who will be hating us?
And if no one is hating us,
then who can be our enemy?
And how can we our enemies
be loving if we have none?
So we should be someone bombing
so we good Christians can be.
I am old, I tell my grandboy, and not understanding this.
I have everywhere in my Bible been looking
even in Second Peter,
and I am not finding these things.
Before, there was only that Thatcher lady
who was like in the Old Testament.
But now her children are everywhere.
I am not minding they are politicians,

but only that their tongues
so much bigger than their brains are.
And then Little Haenschen
is saying Mrs. Thatcher is dead
from that old peoples' disease
and Is this enough pepper
in the soup? and I am with a little spoon slurping
and I am saying, it is too late.
For Mrs Thatcher? he is saying. I know this.
No, I say, I mean, ja, for her, but also
for the pepper it is too late.
You will lots of sour cream be needing
when you are this to your friends serving.
And he is saying that is not good for the heart,
all that cream!
And I must him again be reminding
that even with three full spoons of sour cream
in each bowl his friends will still
from pepper be crying,
and it is good for the heart to be crying.
and it is never for onions and pepper only.
Ja, if we can bone-in-soup be cooking
in a big *Topf*, and with our friends *geschmecking*,
even with lots of cream, and praying *Gott segne uns*,
then, even when our hearts are hurting,
we are healed.

What on TV Was

Oh Doft, mow I am remembering
yesterday I have the pictures on TV
about the war been watching.
Did you also see them,
even if you with the Lord are?
When I the pictures am seeing I remember
one time when I was little still in Russia
in the war, before the unsettling to Canada,
ja, I was maybe five, maybe six years old,
a man to the door was *pummeling*
at night, his hand bleeding in a torn shirt.
He was dirty, I could smell even,
not like the barn smelling, not like pigs
in spring, like old meat more, *Wurst* gone bad.
His eyes were deep like the broken well with no water.
Mutti took him in, and has him soup *gemade*—
Kertofel and water, it was all.
Not real *Bohnensuppe* or borscht even.
I was by the stove scared while he is slurping.
And then Mutti him to the bed showed
where Uncle Peter slept before they took him
and Papa. I was so tight holding
to Mutti's rough wool my fingers were aching.
We were just to bed going then,
the candle *auss-poosting*, and more men came,
krass, loud, shouting even more than you
and Haenschen sometimes.
They grabbed the man from the bed
his feet banging on the floor,
and outside by the barn there was a crash.

The men left and we sat on the bed,
Mutti my hand squeezing again.
Finally with one hand she takes me
and a pail with water in the other,
like she knows what she must do.
Come, Tina, she says, and we walk through the dark
where the cows were—we have them all
eaten, and Fritz the dog also—and there outside
by the door is the man, like a sack.
He is again with dirt and blood *besmeared*
so Mutti takes the water and I too
and we wash him. This could be Papa, she says.
This could somewhere be your Papa.
Always she looks over her shoulder.
I am thinking maybe the men will come back
but I am not afraid. Mutti and I are washing
a man who could be like Papa who was taken away.
Papa's face I can't remember
so I look very close at the dead man's face.
I wonder is he a Kommunist or a Machnovski
or for the Czar or maybe just like Papa.
And now he is just a dead man.
Mutti puts him in Papa's clean white shirt
and upsits him by the wall and we pray:
Lieber Gott what we can
we have done. Now You do.
After, I sleep with Mutti under the blue quilt.
I wonder if the dead man is cold outside.
Have I already you been telling this story?
Anyway, now you already know
because you are with the Lord—
soon I am wanting to come there also.

Every night I am waiting for the train
or the horse wagon even to bring me
to be with the Lord and ja, with you.
But just now I am feeling like talking.
In the morning
I through the shed run to the outside
and the man is gone.
I know God has done something
and I am glad, because maybe he was like Papa.
All my life I carry that inside.
I think your family had already unsettled to Canada.
Maybe even I just remember it now.
But I see on TV the president.
Mr. Bursch and Mr. Saddam
and Schwartzkopf and Yasser, the whole pack of them
they make widows and they blame God, ja?
They want to look strong, because they are cowards.
They are killing so many people.
Ja, I know there are reasons,
always there are reasons to kill, ja?
Always the same.
I am thinking some Mutti
is missing her Papa, and some little Tina somewhere.
Maybe he is dead in the road
or by a shed in the sand. She doesn't know.
And little Tina is afraid but she must clean the body
so God can come and do something.
Sometimes young people see only pictures, ja?
Sometimes I think a good thing
would be if there were bombs in Washington or Ottawa,
then maybe those men would not be so *krass*—
this I can say to you Doft, but not out loud

or they will me send away to Siberia.
Anyway, they are like the pharaoh,
until the firstborn are dead, they will not relent,
and even then, ja, even then,
they will not repent. I have seen this before,
too many times now.

Once you are remembering

there is no stopping the tongue.
So many things I have not told,
that time, did I tell you?
in the bitter Manitoba winter,
the winter with no chinooks?
The ladies at the missionary group
are in our house praying
and when they think I am not hearing
they are stories making up
about our Katie's baby,
who the father is, this man or that man,
the Regehr boy from the hardware store
and why Frieda went to Mexico.
They are talking like this
while they are for relief work mittens knitting
Then I do not want to go back to pray any more.
I go out then to the old chicken house.
In my hand is a fresh egg,
a little cracked,
a little crusty with manure.
I sit in the straw.
Curly feathers, like tiny warm doilies,
around me are slowly falling.
The hens murmur and cluck,
The chickens, they do not judge.

Chicken Soup for the Body

At night-time now I am reading a book Big Haenschen
has me given for Christmas: Chicken Soup for the Soul.
And I am thinking that singing is for the soul
good, but chicken soup is for the body,
and on Sunday we should together
be eating and this idea is me happy making.
Until in the morning I am remembering
that Big Haenschen is busy with Mary-Jean's family
and Katie is in Vancouver
and Frieda has to Mexico gone to help
the poor people.
So Little Haenschen and his Angela
have been coming because they are thinking
maybe to have chickens in the city
in their yard and they want to be learning
from the best cook.
So I am happy.
When you are chicken cooking,
I tell them, it is good the neighbours to be calling
over the fence. If you are dumplings making
there is always enough, like the widow
and Elijah.
The hen your grandboy can be snatching
by the leg with a long pole and a hook on the end.
He will her be dragging and squawking like Elsie Kliewer
singing descant on "What a Friend we Have in Jesus" through the dust.
Then Little Haenschen can both legs hold
and I her neck be stretching across the stump.
The grandboy's Angela is looking away
and her eyes covering when I the axe am lifting

and I tell her she can be praying but
I must my eyes keep open
so I am not my grandboy's arm *ab-geschlachting*
like happened with Pete Friesen once.
Then we can let the body
go around the yard gallivanting
the little red fountains
up-*spritzing* from where her head has been.
When the children still were little, even the girls,
they would laugh and laugh,
and when she wearies from this life
of running running always running,
we *ker-plumpse* her
in a *topf* of boiling water.
After, we in the shade of the big maple tree are sitting
and can hymns be singing when we the feathers
are plucking out. Sometimes in the old days
Frieda was piano playing from the house
so we could hear and sing together:
Ich weiß einen Strom, dessen herrliche Flut
fließt wunderbar stille durchs Land;
doch strahlet und glänzt er wie feurige Glut.
Wem ist dieses Wasser bekannt?
But now, the kids are music in their ears inplugging
their heads bobbing like chickens,
and I am nothing hearing except the ambulance,
sometimes, over by the old folks home.
I am letting Little Haenschen and Angela pinch out
and pull the prickly pin feathers.
They have small fingers, ja.
When they were little
Haenschen and Frieda and even sometimes Katie played

with the skinny feet;
they pulled the muscle strings
from inside their shirt-sleeves,
screaming and laughing to make the fingers move
to scare the cousins from Winnipeg.
When I rinse off the skin I am remembering
how before Katie has off *gelauffen*
with one of the Hardware Rempel boys from Winkler
she could cut the neck and tie off the food tube,
and then pull out the insides.
She used to be liking that,
with the intestines to be playing, slipping them
through her fingers she said, like fat worms,
and finding the heart.
Now Little Haenschen helps me a little,
but his father Big Haenschen and Frieda and Katie—
they are too busy for visiting.
Frieda has told me that in another country
maybe Mexico where she was working once,
they are special soup making
from the chicken insides, but here the *Englische*
even the French ones
just throw this away, or maybe give to the dog.
I am putting the chicken then into a big *Topf*
with the neck, liver, and the heart,
and enough water adding so that she floats.
Then I sprinkle a teaspoon of salt into my hand
and brush it into the pot with my other hand.
When Little Haenschen is the table setting
I am Angela showing how dumplings to be mixing
with flour and milk, and some baking soda,
and then how to make

puffy pillows with the dough
on the hills of chicken above the water.
Then we have time
to call the neighbours again
and our hands to be washing,
and when they are coming in,
the George Hueberts
from church, with three children,
we can put a lid
on the pot just long enough
so I can be praying and the food blessing.
I am with a big *Löffel*
the chicken and dumplings
spooning into our old white plates
with the chips on the edge,
and fresh peas also from the garden.
And Little Haenschen the neck also likes to chew
like his Opa used to. If there were only Mennonites
and no *Englische* we could sing Praise God
from Whom All Blessings Flow
but these neighbours are United Church
even with Mennonite names,
and not singing so good.

After everyone has been home-going
and the yard is dark, the birds are even quiet,

I am thinking to myself that old *Kernlied*[i]
Weißt du, wie viel Sternleinstehen
an dem blauen Himmelszelt?
Weißt du, wie viel Wolken gehen
weithin über alle Welt?
Ach, ja, I am my hands rubbing together

by the window, sitting and singing,
remembering that I must not be forgetting
the chickens to feed before
I am to sleep going.
Okay, I am now going,
Gott segne us.

Acknowledgements

This chapbook-length dramatic monologue has not been previously published in this format.

Earlier fragments and versions of some of this poetry were written as stand-alone pieces in response to particular historical events. Some of these were included in "Mennonite Blues", a stage adaptation created by Larry Danielson in 1984 and performed at a community theatre festival in Morden, Manitoba. Others were included in "Good Housekeeping" (Turnstone, 1983), "Endangered Species" (Turnstone, 1988), "The Impossible Uprooting" (McClelland and Stewart, 1995), and "The Complete Tante Tina: Mennonite Blues and Recipes" (Pandora Press, 2004). An English version of the story of "Chicken Soup for the Body," in English, and not in Tina's voice or from her perspective, was included in the second edition of the nonfiction book "Food, Sex, and Salmonella" (Greystone, 2008). Written from Tina's point of view, it has here become a new and different poem. The section about bean soup has not been published in any format before. Indeed, all of her individual monologues have here been broken apart, re-written and re-arranged to help her, near the end of her life, make sense of it as she talks (mostly) to her late husband, making "Dear Doft" as different from its first fragmented manifestations as a memoir is from a diary.

A Note on Language for Dear Doft

Tante Tina's voice draws, for both words and syntax, on high German, (which God spoke, and which the Mennonite community I grew up in used for education and religion, that is, high culture), and Low German, which is rooted in an oral, rather than a written, tradition. Low German (*plautdietsch*, or, literally, Flat German), comes originally from the flat lands of Northern Germany, Friesland, and The Netherlands, and was carried along as a functional "mother tongue" as Mennonites migrated across Europe, into the Russian Empire, and finally around the world. It was a language used on the farm, for down-to-earth real-life conversations, and which my parents used to keep secrets from us children. Thus, while I picked up the rhythm of the tongue, I cannot myself speak it.

If you want to find out more about this stuff, track down a Mennonite whose ancestors migrated over from the Ukraine sometime in the last century - people with names like Friesen, Reimer, Rempel, Toews and Thiessen. There are a lot of them in southern Manitoba. I'd send you to books, of which there are a few, but this is one case where books can never do the language justice. You really need to talk to someone. The same holds true for the songs used in the poems. You can see some of them in Mennonite hymnals, but you'll be better off (and no doubt a better person) hearing them sung in four-part harmony. Visit a local Mennonite Church; check ahead to make sure they're the singing kind (some of them aren't). There's really no substitute for the real thing.

About the Author

David Waltner-Toews is a veterinary epidemiologist and University Professor Emeritus at the University of Guelph. He was founding president of Veterinarians without Borders / Vétérinaires sans Frontières – Canada (www.vetswithoutborders.ca/) and a founding member of Communities of Practice for Ecosystem Approaches to Health in Canada (www.copeh-canada.org). In 2010 the International Association for Ecology and Health presented him with the inaugural award for contributions to ecosystem approaches to health, and in 2019 he received an award from the World Small Animal Veterinary Association recognizing "veterinarians who have exhibited exceptional acts of valour and commitment in the face of adversity to service the community." In 2022 he was appointed as an Officer in Order of Canada, where he was cited "for his leadership and expertise in ecosystem approaches to health, and for supporting development worldwide."

Previous Books by the same Author

Selected Poetry

The Gravity of Love, St.Thomas Poetry Series, November 18, 2023

The Complete Tante Tina: Mennonite Blues and Recipes, Pandora Press, Kitchener, 2004

The Fat Lady Struck Dumb, Brick Books, London, Ontario, 2000

The Impossible Uprooting, McClelland & Stewart, Toronto, 1995.

Endangered Species, Turnstone Press, Winnipeg, 1988.

Three Mennonite Poets, with Jean Janzen and Yorifume Yaguchi, Good Books, 1986.

Good Housekeeping, Turnstone Press, Winnipeg, 1983.

The Earth is One Body, Turnstone Press, Winnipeg, 1979.

That Inescapable Animal, Pinchpenny Press, Goshen, Indiana, 1974.

Selected Nonfiction

A Conspiracy of Chickens: a memoir (Wolsak & Wynn, 2022)

On Pandemics: Deadly Diseases from Bubonic Plague to Coronavirus. (Greystone Books, 2020)

Eat the Beetles! An Exploration into our Conflicted Relationship with Insects. (ECW, 2017; IPPY Gold Medal winner).

The Origin of Feces: what excrement tells us about evolution, ecology and a sustainable society (ECW, 2013; IPPY Silver Medal).

Food, Sex, and Salmonella: Why our food is making us sick. (Greystone Books, 2008).

The Chickens Fight Back: Pandemic Panics and Deadly Diseases that Jump from Animals to Humans. (Greystone Books, 2007). Short-listed, Canadian Science Writers Award.

Ecosystem Sustainability and Health: a practical approach. Cambridge University Press. 2004.

One Animal Among Many: Gaia, Goats and Garlic. NC Press, Toronto, 1991.

[1] Or because he already had a wife and child who did not want to leave. After a life as a machinist, blacksmith, school administrator, and army draftee, Gerhard, his wife Katharine and daughter Frieda were able to emigrate to Canada in 1948.

[2] We always referred to ourselves as Russian Mennonites, because we had settled there at the invitation of the Russian empress Catherine the Great and when my parents fled it was the Soviet Union (ie the new Russian empire). However my Ukrainian friends point out—quite rightly—that the Mennonite colonies were in what is now called Ukraine, so now, when I remember, I put "Russian" into quotation marks.

[3] Nick Lindsay was included in Studs Terkel's collection of interviews with American workers, *Working: People talk about what they do all day and how they feel about what they do* (New York: Pantheon Books, 1973)

[4] Graeme, who died in 2019, was also Margaret Atwood's partner.

[5] The woman was Marjorie Doyle who in 2016 was elected Chair of TWUC.

[6] Pronounced "Zo Vahs"

[7] Pronounced "zaht"

[i] According to celebrated Canadian conductor and radio broadcaster Howard Dyck (son-in-law to my aunt Truda, whom I mentioned in the preface), *Kernlieder*, or "core songs," were the brainchild of Manitoba musician Ben Horch. Horch assembled a list of hymns which he regarded as seminal to the Mennonite Brethren experience. These hymns have differing origins: English Methodist, American Gospel, and some German Protestant. A number of these *Kernlieder* are quoted in Victor Davies's Mennonite Piano Concerto. I (DWT) grew up thinking of them as sort of "folk" songs which, in a sort of way, I suppose they were. This particular song, about God's counting, naming, and taking pleasure in stars, clouds, fish and children, is based on a German folk melody, with words by German pastor, fabulist and poet Wilhelm Hey in 1837.